Hea

BREAKFASTS UNDER 300 CALORIES

That Keep You Feeling Energized and Help You Lose Weight

Corina Tudose

2012

To my Grandparents.

Table of Contents

Preface

Breakfast is the most important meal of the day! It is one of the make-it or break-it of a healthy weight loss or weight maintenance plan. A healthy breakfast fuels the body and provides the foundation for a balanced day. Much like a domino effect, starting the day off right, will help you eat healthy, balanced meals all throughout. So do yourself the biggest favor, and promise yourself never to skip breakfast again (this book will help you keep that promise)!

While it's extremely important to eat breakfast, it is just as important to eat foods that are natural, nutritious and full of vitamins. Fatty, processed foods do not keep your body fueled and in fact they leave you wanting more. The best food sources in the AM hours are whole grains, fruits, vegetables, nuts and seeds. The right type of combinations can help you stay full, energized and ready to face even the busiest day! And this is exactly what this book is all about!

If you have struggled with finding the right recipes for breakfast, you can finally breathe in relief. These great breakfasts are full of nutrition, healthy ingredients and taste simply scrumptious. No more hidden fats, sugars, and mystery ingredients. All these recipes are made with fresh, natural ingredients and items that you always have around your healthy kitchen and in your pantry. Plus, more than half of the recipes take less than 10 minutes to make. Achieving your healthy and weight loss goals has never been easier.

Delicious and filling, these recipes give you all the nutritional information you need in order to make an informed decision: protein content, fiber, carbs and cholesterol, it's all here. Plus each serving is _300 calories or less_, so no worries there! For the readers following the Weight Watchers® program, the Weight Watchers Points Plus® points are also included, which means even more reasons why eating a balanced breakfast just got easier!

So what can you expect? A variety of delicious smoothies and creamy parfaits, such as the "Power Kick Crunchy Smoothie" and "Pumpkin Pie Taste-Alike Parfait." They are sure to become a household favorite. The "Be Mine Blueberry Cake" is one of our most praised and requested recipes. It's sometimes hard to believe that this cake is actually _HEALTHY_! And if you love French toast, you will ADORE the "Healthy Frenchy" recipe. It has all the great flavors of a childhood brunch, minus the fatty calories. But, don't take our word for it, give it a try yourself!

In case the all natural ingredients, complete nutritional info and low calorie options were not enough, we divided the recipes in two easy-to-follow categories: **10 minutes or less** and _15 minutes or more_.

The 10 minutes or less options are perfect for those days when you literally need to get up and go. The 15 minutes or more are reserved for laid back weekends or make ahead treats. Even so, no recipe takes longer than 55 minutes to make, so you are sure to find the one that best suits your time and taste!

Bon Appétit!

Corina Tudose

Healthy Breakfasts Ready in 10 Minutes or Less

The Parfait Breakfast for the Perfect Day

This great and super easy breakfast is perfect for those mornings when you are in a hurry but still want to eat something healthy. Plus it is rich in vitamins and other great nutrients which will fill you up with energy for the entire day!

General Information:

Difficulty Level: *Easy*

Preparation Time: *0 min*

Cooking Time: *5 min*

Total Time Needed: *5 min*

Estimated Total Servings: *1*

Nutrition Facts:

Amount per serving:

Calories: *244*

Total Fat: *4.1 g*

Cholesterol: *14 mg*

Sodium: *693 mg*

Carbohydrate: *38 g*

Protein: *26.1 g*

Fiber: *4.6 g*

WW PointsPlus®: *7*

What You Need:

3/4 cup low-fat cottage cheese (or low-fat plain yogurt)

2 teaspoons toasted wheat germ

1/2 cup pineapple chunks

1/2 cup papaya slices

How to Make It:

Spoon the yogurt or the cottage cheese in a small bowl. Sprinkle it with the toasted wheat germ. (You can toast it yourself in case it is not already toasted. Simply place it on a wax paper-lined tray and place it in the oven on medium heat for 10 minutes.) Then add the chunks of fruit and enjoy immediately, to make sure the wheat germ does not get soggy from the yogurt and the fruit juices.

Tip: To turn this great breakfast into a delicious afternoon snack, reduce the quantity of cottage cheese/ yogurt and fruit to half and replace the wheat germ with crushed nuts such as almonds or pecans.

Spice Up Your Morning Pita Pocket

A delicious and super fast recipe, this breakfast pita pocket is extremely versatile. You can add all the healthy vegetables you adore (try green onions, tomatoes and bell peppers) and get your energy boost for the day in just 10 minutes!

General Information:

Difficulty Level: *Easy*

Preparation Time: *0 min*

Cooking Time: *10 min*

Total Time Needed: *10 min*

Estimated Total Servings: *1*

Nutrition Facts:

Amount per serving:

Calories: *226*

Total Fat: *10.4 g*

Cholesterol: *201 mg*

Sodium: *453 mg*

Carbohydrate: *17.7 g*

Protein: *16.2 g*

Fiber: *2.6 g*

WW PointsPlus®: *6*

What You Need:

1 large egg

1 egg white

1 whole wheat pita

1 Tablespoon medium salsa

2 Tablespoons shredded reduced-fat Cheddar cheese

How to Make It:

Grease a small pan using cooking spray and set it over medium heat. Beat the egg and egg white together in a medium bowl and pour the mixture in the pan. Cook it, stirring occasionally, for about 1-2 minutes or until it is cooked to your liking. When the eggs are done, reduce the heat to low and sprinkle the Cheddar cheese on top. Cover the pan with a lid and let the cheese melt for 3-4 minutes.

Cut the pita in half so that you get two half circle pockets. Divide the cooked eggs evenly between the two sides. Layer the salsa over the eggs and serve warm.

Tip: To go all natural, try using homemade salsa. Simply chop half a tomato, half of green chili pepper (seeded) and 1 teaspoon of lime juice - you can easily do that while the eggs are cooking. It's the perfect combination for those who love a spicy kick in the morning!

Smokey-Hot Salmon and Eggs Breakfast

Flavorful, healthy, filled with protein and vitamins, plus quick to make - this could definitely be the perfect breakfast! Enjoy its great taste and feel great the whole day through.

General Information:

Difficulty Level: *Easy*

Preparation Time: *0 min*

Cooking Time: *10 min*

Total Time Needed: *10 min*

Estimated Total Servings: *1*

Nutrition Facts:

Amount per serving:

Calories: *221*

Total Fat: *4.6 g*

Cholesterol: *7 mg*

Sodium: *117 mg*

Carbohydrate: *24.2 g*

Protein: *17.7 g*

Fiber: *3 g*

WW PointsPlus®: *5*

What You Need:

1/2 teaspoon extra-virgin olive oil

1 Tablespoon finely chopped red onion

1/2 teaspoon capers, rinsed (optional)

2 large egg whites, beaten

Pinch of salt

1 ounce smoked salmon

1 slice tomato

1 whole-wheat English muffin, split and toasted

How to Make It:

Lightly grease a small pan with the olive oil and set it over medium heat. Place the onion in the pan and cook it about 1-2 minutes until it begins to soften. Add the capers, egg whites and salt and cook them for approximately 2 minutes, stirring constantly using a wooden spatula.

Layer the cooked egg whites, then add the smoked salmon and the tomato on the English muffin and enjoy it while it is warm.

Tip: *To turn this nutritious breakfast into a great evening snack or even dinner, use poached salmon instead of the smoked one and replace the muffin with whole wheat baguette.*

Power Kick Crunchy Smoothie

There is nothing healthier or better suited for breakfast than a refreshing, nutritious drink that you can whip up in minutes. Treat your kids with this delicious fruit smoothie to give them a blast of vitamins, protein and calcium! Come to think of it, everyone needs a bit of that so treat everyone in the family, regardless of their age!

General Information:

Difficulty Level: *Easy*

Preparation Time: *0 min*

Cooking Time: *3 min*

Total Time Needed: *3 min*

Estimated Total Servings: *2*

Nutrition Facts:

Amount per serving:

Calories: *131*

Total Fat: *4.3 g*

Cholesterol: *2 mg*

Sodium: *38 mg*

Carbohydrate: *20.2 g*

Protein: *5.3 g*

Fiber: *3.7 g*

WW PointsPlus®: *3*

What You Need:

1/2 cup frozen peaches

1 orange, peeled

1/2 cup 2% plain yogurt

1/2 cup water

12 almonds, crushed or slivered

How to Make It:

Put the peaches, orange, yogurt and water in a food processor or blender and process the mixture until it has reached a smooth consistency for about 2 minutes. Transfer it into two glasses and blend in half of the almonds in each glass. Enjoy!

Tip: This smoothie tastes as fantastic if you replace the yogurt with almond milk and add a dash of vanilla extract. It's the perfect start of the day for those who are lactose intolerant or those who do not like milk products.

The Perfect Date Oatmeal

This easy to make oatmeal recipe is perfect for you and your morning sweet craving. Not to mention that your kids will surely love it too. The cocoa and date combination gives this dish an amazing flavor and the right amount of sweetness. No added sugar or any artificial sweeteners, which means it is good for your health too!

General Information:

Difficulty Level: *Easy*

Preparation Time: *0 min*

Cooking Time: *10 min*

Total Time Needed: *10 min*

Estimated Total Servings: *4*

Nutrition Facts:

Amount per serving:

Calories: *265*

Total Fat: *4.3 g*

Cholesterol: *0 mg*

Sodium: *86 mg*

Carbohydrate: *51.6 g*

Protein: *8.5 g*

Fiber: *8.4 g*

WW PointsPlus®: *7*

What You Need:

1 cup old-fashioned rolled oats

1/4 cup chopped pitted dates, (10-12 dates)

2 Tablespoons cocoa

Pinch of salt

2 cups water

How to Make It:

Place the oats, dates, cocoa and salt in a 1-quart microwave resistant dish. Carefully stir in 2 cups of water and partially cover the dish with a resistant lid. Set the microwave to medium heat and cook the mixture for 3-4 minutes then stir it well. Cook it for another 4 minutes in the microwave on medium heat then stir and repeat until the oatmeal has reached a creamy consistency. It should not take more than 10 minutes overall.

Tip: Love dates but would like an extra kick? Try adding a pinch of cinnamon, vanilla and nutmeg and enjoy a stronger taste.

No Shell Taco-Style Omelet

This is such a great way to include healthy seasonal vegetables right at the beginning of the day. Their fiber will keep you fueled up for hours! Feel free to experiment with your favorite veggies and enjoy this delicious and nutritious omelet the way you love it best.

General Information:

Difficulty Level: *Medium*

Preparation Time: *5 min*

Cooking Time: *5 min*

Total Time Needed: *10 min*

Estimated Total Servings: *1*

Nutrition Facts:

Amount per serving:

Calories: *257*

Total Fat: *9.8 g*

Cholesterol: *32 mg*

Sodium: *1000 mg*

Carbohydrate: *24.4 g*

Protein: *22.1 g*

Fiber: *4.0 g*

WW PointsPlus®: *7*

What You Need:

Cooking spray

1/2 cup chopped zucchini

3 Tablespoons chopped green onions

2/3 cup frozen whole-kernel corn, thawed

1/4 teaspoon salt, divided

3 large egg whites

1/4 teaspoon black pepper

2 Tablespoons water

2 Tablespoons shredded smoked Gouda cheese

How to Make It:

Lightly grease a pan using cooking spray and set it over medium heat. Place the zucchini, onions, corn and 1/6 teaspoon salt in the pan and sauté them until they begin to tender (that should take about 3-4 minutes). Set aside.

Place the egg whites, 1/8 teaspoon salt, pepper and water in a small bowl and whisk thoroughly.

Lightly grease a skillet using cooking spray and set it over medium heat, pour the egg mixture and cook for about 2 minutes or until the edges begin to set and slightly brown. Use a spatula to carefully lift the edges of the omelet, allowing the unset mixture to shift and come in contact with the hot skillet. Spread the vegetable mixture on one half of the omelet and top it with the shredded Gouda cheese. Using the spatula, lift the other half of the omelet and fold it over the vegetables and cheese. Allow the omelet to cook for 2-3 more minutes - the cheese should melt. Transfer to a plate and serve warm alongside a piece of whole wheat toast.

Tip: This delicious and easy to make recipe is extremely easy to "spice up". So go ahead and try using low fat mozzarella cheese instead of Gouda or try mixing up the vegetables with other ones - how about mushrooms, spinach, bell peppers? Adding some crushed red pepper flakes and paprika to the onion mixture will give the dish an amazing kick of flavor!

The 5 Minute Home Made Muesli

Sweet, fruity, nutty and nutritious - a tasty breakfast dish that has it all! You and your kids are going to love this great combination of yogurt, honey, berries and almonds!

General Information:
Difficulty Level: *Easy*

Preparation Time: *0 min*

Cooking Time: *5 min*

Total Time Needed: *5 min (+overnight refrigeration)*

Estimated Total Servings: *6*

Nutrition Facts:
Amount per serving:

Calories: *262*

Total Fat: *12.2 g*

Cholesterol: *3 mg*

Sodium: *46 mg*

Carbohydrate: *29.4 g*

Protein: *10.8 g*

Fiber: *4.7 g*

WW PointsPlus®: *7*

What You Need:

1/2 cup unsalted raw almonds

1 cup nonfat plain yogurt

1 cup nonfat milk

2 Tablespoons raw honey

1 cup old-fashioned rolled oats

1/4 teaspoon vanilla extract

1/2 cup blueberries

1 cup strawberries

How to Make It:

Place a skillet over high heat and toast the almonds until they become golden and deliciously fragrant - it should take about 4-5 minutes - then chop them coarsely.

Place the yogurt, milk, honey, oats and vanilla extract in a bowl and blend them together. Refrigerate overnight.

Evenly spread the oats mixture into 6 small bowls (or parfait dishes, if you have them) then top each of them with 1/6 of the mixed berries and 2 tablespoons of chopped almonds.

Tip: *This delicious breakfast treat is the perfect grab and go meal. All you need to do is mix the ingredients the night before. This way the morning preparation takes less than 1 minute. And it can be stored in an air tight container in the refrigerator for up to 3 days! If you forget to prep it overnight, replace the oats with wheat germ for a perfect on the spot parfait.*

Energy Fix Spicy Omelet Wrap

This delicious breakfast dish is easy to make and filled with protein, so it will keep you energized all through the day. Once you have tasted it you might want to cook up a double portion: one for breakfast and one portion to take it with you for lunch!

General Information:

Difficulty Level: *Medium*

Preparation Time: *2 min*

Cooking Time: *5 min*

Total Time Needed: *7 min*

Estimated Total Servings: *1*

Nutrition Facts:

Amount per serving:

Calories: *243*

Total Fat: *12.4 g*

Cholesterol: *15 mg*

Sodium: *606 mg*

Carbohydrate: *26.7 g*

Protein: *16 g*

Fiber: *8.4 g*

WW PointsPlus®: *7*

What You Need:

2 large egg whites

Freshly ground pepper, to taste

1/2 teaspoon hot sauce

1 Tablespoon chopped scallions

1 Tablespoon chopped fresh cilantro, or parsley (optional)

2 Tablespoons grated pepper Jack or Cheddar cheese

1 teaspoon olive oil

1 8-inch whole-wheat wrap

1 leaf romaine lettuce

How to Make It:

Place the egg whites, pepper and hot sauce in a small bowl and whisk them thoroughly, then add the scallions, cilantro and 1 tablespoon of the cheese and mix well.

Lightly grease a small (6-inch) non-stick skillet with the olive oil, set it over medium heat and pour in the egg mixture. Cook until the edges are set, about 3 minutes. Then gently lift the eggs with a spatula to allow the uncooked mixture to slide underneath and come in contact with the hot skillet. Cook until the bottom is golden - no more than an additional 30-40 seconds.

In a grill or microwave slightly heat the wrap for 30 seconds. Sprinkle the remaining cheese on the wrap then add the omelet on top. Place the lettuce leaf on top of the omelet. Roll the wrap and fold the edges inside to hold it in place. Cut it in half and serve immediately.

Tip: This is a great breakfast dish that you can make ahead of time! Follow the steps described in the recipe for cooking the eggs the night before. Refrigerate the dish, then in the morning heat it up in the microwave for 1-2 minutes, add the lettuce and wrap and you are all set.

Go Bananas Dairy-Free Smoothie

Delicious, refreshing and super healthy - this smoothie is a great combination of taste, nutritional value and an all in all wise choice for a healthy breakfast. Enjoy it with your family on a sunny Sunday morning or whenever a little chocolate craving crawls in!

General Information:

Difficulty Level: *Easy*

Preparation Time: *1 min*

Cooking Time: *1 min*

Total Time Needed: *2 min*

Estimated Total Servings: *1*

Nutrition Facts:

Amount per serving:

Calories: *235*

Total Fat: *5.1 g*

Cholesterol: *0 mg*

Sodium: *68 mg*

Carbohydrate: *46.9 g*

Protein: *9.2 g*

Fiber: *7.1 g*

WW PointsPlus®: *7*

What You Need:

1 organic banana

1/2 cup organic plain soy milk

30 g water-packed silken tofu

1 teaspoon raw honey

1 square (3 g) of 70% dark chocolate

How to Make It:

Slice up the banana, and put it in a food processor. Add the soy milk, tofu, honey and chocolate and blend on pulse for about 1 minute, until the mixture has a smooth consistency.

Tip: If you have no dairy restrictions you can substitute the soy milk with 2% milk and the tofu with fat free yogurt. It will give you the same great taste plus a boost of calcium!

Pumpkin Pie Taste-Alike Parfait

Quick to make and quick to disappear off the table - that's how good this parfait is! Sweet and nutritious, it is also a healthy choice for breakfast. Your kids will love how much it resembles pumpkin pie filling and you will love that you can finally enjoy flavor without pilling on the calories!

General Information:

Difficulty Level: *Easy*

Preparation Time: *5 min*

Cooking Time: *0 min*

Total Time Needed: *5 min*

Estimated Total Servings: *2*

Nutrition Facts:

Amount per serving:

Calories: *219*

Total Fat: *11.6 g*

Cholesterol: *7 mg*

Sodium: *87 mg*

Carbohydrate: *19.8 g*

Protein: *8.5 g*

Fiber: *2.0 g*

WW PointsPlus®: *6*

What You Need:

2 teaspoons raw honey

1 cup plain low-fat yogurt

1/4 teaspoon pumpkin-pie spice blend

10 pecans, chopped

1/2 cup papaya, chopped in 1-inch pieces

How to Make It:

Place the honey, yogurt and pumpkin pie spice in a bowl and blend them together. Divide the yogurt mix in two parfait cups. Layer the yogurt mixture, with the papaya chunks and sprinkle pecans on top.

Tip: If you are looking for a delicious treat but want to cut down the calories further, simply leave out the honey. To get an extra kick of flavor replace it with one teaspoon of vanilla extract or maple extract. You will get a creamy and delicious treat that will also satisfy your sweet tooth.

Hot and Spicy Breakfast

Easy to make, chock full of proteins and tasty! Should we say more? This amazing egg dish is definitely going to be one of your go-to recipes for a healthy, quick and delicious breakfast.

General Information:

Difficulty Level: *Easy*

Preparation Time: *2 min*

Cooking Time: *3 min*

Total Time Needed: *5 min*

Estimated Total Servings: *1*

Nutrition Facts:

Amount per serving:

Calories: *237*

Total Fat: *8.8 g*

Cholesterol: *0 mg*

Sodium: *276 mg*

Carbohydrate: *32.5 g*

Protein: *14.2 g*

Fiber: *11.6 g*

WW PointsPlus®: *6*

What You Need:

5 cherry tomatoes

2 scallions

1 teaspoon hot sauce

1/4 avocado

2 large egg whites

1 Tablespoon fresh lemon juice

How to Make It:

Cut each tomato in 4 slices and set aside. Chop the scallions and toss them with the hot sauce. Slice the avocado in thin wedges, you should get approximately 4 pieces.

Set a medium sized non-stick pan over high heat. Once it is well heated, place the eggs directly into the pan. Cook for about 1 minute on one side, turn the eggs and cover the pan. Cook for another 2 minutes. Place the eggs on a plate and top them with the cherry tomatoes, scallions, avocado and drizzle the lemon juice on top.

Best served hot, with crispy baked whole-wheat toast.

Tip: To build an entire meal around this great dish and turn it into a great tasting lunch, simply serve it alongside a large crunchy spring mix salad. It makes for a super light and delicious meal! Double or triple the ingredients and you can make a super delicious breakfast to feed the entire family in just 5 minutes!

Popeye-Approved Spinach Omelet

A great way to include vitamins, proteins and... amazing taste in your breakfast, this delicious omelet is both light and satisfying. It will keep you well fed and energetic, to conquer a busy morning!

General Information:

Difficulty Level: *Easy*

Preparation Time: *1 min*

Cooking Time: *4 min*

Total Time Needed: *5 min*

Estimated Total Servings: *1*

Nutrition Facts:

Amount per serving:

Calories: *181*

Total Fat: *10.1 g*

Cholesterol: *184 mg*

Sodium: *435 mg*

Carbohydrate: *1.9 g*

Protein: *19.6 g*

Fiber: *0.7 g*

WW PointsPlus®: *5*

What You Need:

1 egg

2 egg whites

2 slices *cooked* turkey bacon, crumbled

1 cup baby spinach, washed and rinsed

1 teaspoon olive oil

How to Make It:

Whisk the egg and egg whites together in a medium sized bowl. Add the bacon and spinach and blend well. Lightly grease a pan with the olive oil, set over medium heat and cook the egg mixture for 1-2 minutes. Using a spatula flip the eggs over (do not worry if the omelet breaks, just make sure to turn all pieces). Cook for another 1-2 minutes. Serve the omelet on buttered toast (if you are allowed to splurge a little) or next to tomato slices.

Tip: To avoid the added calories from the bacon, replace it with 10 red grapes. They will give this dish a sweet and exotic taste!

Cooler than Cool Vegan Breakfast Smoothie

Refreshing and filled with vitamins that will keep you energized the whole day through! This is a delicious drink that you can enjoy every morning and be sure that you have made a super healthy choice.

General Information:

Difficulty Level: *Easy*

Preparation Time: *1 min*

Cooking Time: *3 min*

Total Time Needed: *4 min*

Estimated Total Servings: *2*

Nutrition Facts:

Amount per serving:

Calories: *107*

Total Fat: *0.5 g*

Cholesterol: *0 mg*

Sodium: *11 mg*

Carbohydrate: *27.4 g*

Protein: *1.2 g*

Fiber: *5.6 g*

WW PointsPlus®: *3*

What You Need:

2 green apples

1 cup chopped peeled seedless cucumber (about 1/2 pound)

10 ice cubes (about 4 oz)

1/4 cup cold water

1/4 cup chopped fresh mint

How to Make It:

Place the apples, chopped cucumber, chopped mint, ices cubes and water in a blender or a food processor and blend for about 2-3 minutes or until the mixture reaches a smooth consistency. Serve immediately and garnish it with chopped fresh mint.

Tip: Why not turn this delicious breakfast into a fancy party beverage? Make it on the spot, garnish it elegantly with a lemon wedge and mint and serve it to your friends before dinner or as a welcome drink to a baby shower! All your guests will be impressed and they will surely fall in love with its great freshness and taste.

Do-It-Yourself Orange-Flavored Yogurt

This easy recipe gives you the chance to make your own orange-flavored yogurt; it is a great choice for a healthy all natural breakfast or snack. What could possibly be better for starting off the day right?

General Information:

Difficulty Level: *Easy*

Preparation Time: *5 min*

Cooking Time: *5 min*

Total Time Needed: *10 min*

Estimated Total Servings: *4*

Nutrition Facts:

Amount per serving:

Calories: *276*

Total Fat: *7.1 g*

Cholesterol: *11 mg*

Sodium: *130 mg*

Carbohydrate: *37.3 g*

Protein: *13.9 g*

Fiber: *4.2 g*

WW PointsPlus®: *7*

What You Need:

3 cups plain low-fat yogurt

2 oranges

1/4 cup chopped walnuts

1/4 cup raisins

1 orange, peeled, zest grated

1 1/2 teaspoons pure vanilla extract

Orange, orange zest, raisins and walnuts, for garnish

How to Make It:

Drain the water out of the yogurt. Place the yogurt and oranges in a food processor and blend well for about 1 minute.

In a medium bowl mix together the walnuts, raisins, orange zest and vanilla extract. Stir well and add to the yogurt mix. Make sure the ingredients are well blended. Garnish with pieces of orange, raisins and/or walnuts and serve in individual bowls.

Tip: This dish keeps well in the refrigerator. Prepare the orange-flavored yogurt as described above and store in the refrigerator for a few days, ready to be enjoyed for breakfast or as a healthy snack anytime.

Gingery Cantaloupe Treat

Refreshing and super easy to make, this tasty cantaloupe dish is great for starting the morning off right! But, as you will surely come to realize, it is an easy way to impress guests, so it is a great choice for an appetizer for your next party.

General Information:

Difficulty Level: *Easy*

Preparation Time: *0 min*

Cooking Time: *5 min*

Total Time Needed: *5 min*

Estimated Total Servings: *1*

Nutrition Facts:

Amount per serving:

Calories: *198*

Total Fat: *0.7 g*

Cholesterol: *0 mg*

Sodium: *16 mg*

Carbohydrate: *48.7 g*

Protein: *2.5 g*

Fiber: *1.9 g*

WW PointsPlus®: *6*

What You Need:

1/2 cantaloupe, sliced into wedges

3 Tablespoons raw honey

1-inch piece fresh ginger, peeled and finely grated

Small handful fresh mint leaves (approximately half a cup)

How to Make It:

Place the cantaloupe slices on a serving platter and arrange them into a circular flower, using the wedges as the petals. Using a teaspoon, pour the honey in zigzag shapes over the cantaloupe wedges.

Remove the excess juice from the ginger and sprinkle over the cantaloupe. Garnish with freshly cut mint. To get a fancier look place the mint in the middle of the "flower". Serve immediately or if you have the time chill the arrangement for 30-40 minutes in the refrigerator. This will make the dish even more flavorful.

Tip: Looking for an out-of-the-box twist? Try sprinkling some coconut flakes and ¼ teaspoon kosher salt over the cantaloupe. The sweet and savory combination and the exotic taste of the coconut will make your taste buds go wild!

Healthy Breakfasts Ready in 15 Minutes or More

Wrap Me Up and Go Scramble

Nutritious and super fast to make, these delicious wraps are a great choice for those mornings when you are in a hurry. If you crave a good, light meal that will fill you up with vitamins and energy and keep you going all day long, this is your go-to recipe!

General Information:

Difficulty Level: *Medium*

Preparation Time: *10 min*

Cooking Time: *5 min*

Total Time Needed: *15 min*

Estimated Total Servings: *4*

Nutrition Facts:

Amount per serving:

Calories: *226*

Total Fat: *6.3 g*

Cholesterol: *86 mg*

Sodium: *708 mg*

Carbohydrate: *33.0 g*

Protein: *11.5 g*

Fiber: *4.2 g*

WW PointsPlus®: *6*

What You Need:

For the scrambled eggs:

2 eggs

4 egg whites

Coarse salt and cracked black pepper, to taste

1/2 teaspoon extra-virgin olive oil

Salsa Verde:

1 (13-ounce) can tomatillos or 6 medium peeled and cored tomatillos, cut into quarters

1/2 cup loosely packed cilantro leaves

1/4 jalapeno, seeded and cut into several pieces

1/2 lime, juiced

1/2 teaspoon coarse salt

1/8 cup water

4 (6-inch) whole-wheat flour tortillas

How to Make It:

Place the eggs and egg white in a bowl and whisk them together then season with salt and pepper to taste. Lightly grease a skillet with olive oil and set it over medium heat. Cook the eggs for about 1 minute then, using a heatproof spatula, stir them gently until they are cooked through.

To make the salsa: place the tomatillos, cilantro leaves, jalapeno, lime, salt and water in a food processor or blender. Use the pulse function to process until the mixture becomes smooth. (If the sauce is too thick for your liking you may add water until it reaches the desired consistency.

Heat up the flour tortillas in a microwave or in a pan, divide the cooked eggs evenly and top each of the 4 wraps with salsa. Roll the tortillas and secure one end using aluminum foil. Enjoy them while they are warm.

Tip: *To turn this quick and easy breakfast into a great lunch simply add 1 chopped green onion and 1 tablespoon low-fat crumbled feta cheese to the eggs and serve alongside a healthy salad with all your favorite vegetables.*

Nut Lover's Paradise

An amazing and super easy way to make a nutritious and satisfying breakfast. Using only natural ingredients, this great recipe will help you and your loved ones get a ton of energy. Eating breakfast just got easier!

General Information:

Difficulty Level: *Medium*

Preparation Time: *0 min*

Cooking Time: *35 min*

Total Time Needed: *35 min*

Estimated Total Servings: *6*

Nutrition Facts:

Amount per serving:

Calories: *297*

Total Fat: *12.1 g*

Cholesterol: *0 mg*

Sodium: *7 mg*

Carbohydrate: *42.7 g*

Protein: *7.4 g*

Fiber: *6.6 g*

WW PointsPlus®: *8*

What You Need:

1/3 cup ground flaxseed

1/4 cup chopped walnuts

1/4 cup chopped almonds

2 cups regular oats

2 teaspoons ground cinnamon

1/4 cup honey

1/3 cup freshly squeezed orange juice

1/4 cup brown sugar

2 teaspoons canola oil

1 teaspoon vanilla extract

Cooking spray

1/3 cup dried cranberries (optional)

How to Make It:

Place the ground flaxseeds, chopped walnuts and almonds, oats and cinnamon in a medium sized bowl and mix them together.

Put the honey, orange juice and brown sugar in a small saucepan and cook over low to medium heat until the sugar is completely dissolved, about 3-4 minutes. Remember to stir often, or else the sugar becomes caramelized. If it becomes too sticky you can add 1-2 tablespoons of water. Once the sugar is dissolved, remove the pan from heat and stir in the canola oil and the vanilla extract.

Pour the honey and sugar mixture over the dry ingredients and stir well until the cereal and nuts are well coated with the honey mixture.

Preheat the oven to 300 degrees F (150 degrees C) and lightly grease a jelly-roll pan with cooking spray. Spoon the mixture into the pan and spread it evenly in a thin layer. Bake it for 10 minutes then take it out of the oven, shake it well and bake for 10-15 more minutes or until the mixture becomes golden-brown.

Let it cool for 5 minutes then add the dried cranberries. Stir well and serve with ½ cup of low-fat milk or low-fat yogurt.

Tip: This delicious granola keeps wonderfully; you can make it ahead of time, store it in an air tight container and enjoy it for up to 2 weeks. Also, if you like your granola crunchier and less sticky, you can remove the honey all together and replace it with water.

Fruity Grilled Cheese Sandwich

A lavish breakfast or festive brunch, these amazingly creamy and sweet sandwiches are a great treat for your family or guests. They are designed to become a house favorite and you can enjoy them wholeheartedly, as they are both delicious and nutritious.

General Information:

Difficulty Level: *Easy*

Preparation Time: *5 min*

Cooking Time: *10 min*

Total Time Needed: *15 min*

Estimated Total Servings: *4*

Nutrition Facts:

Amount per serving:

Calories: *184*

Total Fat: *5.4 g*

Cholesterol: *11 mg*

Sodium: *294 mg*

Carbohydrate: *26.2 g*

Protein: *8.1 g*

Fiber: *4.1 g*

WW PointsPlus®: *5*

What You Need:

1/4 teaspoon grated lemon rind

4 Tablespoons low-fat cream cheese

1 Tablespoon golden raisins

1 teaspoon cinnamon powder

8 slices whole wheat bread

4 Tablespoons grated green apples

How to Make It:

Place the lemon rind, cheese, raisins, and cinnamon in a bowl and mix them together. Take 4 slices of bread and spread 1 tablespoon of the mixture on each. Top each slice with 1 tablespoon of grated apples. Complete the sandwiches by topping with the other 4 slices of bread. Press them well together.

Set a non-stick large pan over medium to high heat. Put 2 of the sandwiches in the pan and place a large cast-iron skillet on top of them, thus pressing them down while they cook.

Cook the sandwiches for 2-3 minutes on each side - until the bread looks lightly toasted. Repeat these steps for all sandwiches and serve them warm.

Tip: To turn this great dish into an appetizer, divide the spread mixture in 8 parts. Spread it over each piece of bread and cook the sandwiches "open-faced" style. Top each slice with fresh berries (instead of the apples) and some fresh mint leaves. The taste will be amazing and the display will be even more appealing.

Berrilicious Wheat Germ Muffins

Super healthy and easy to make, these great muffins are a delicious and nutritious breakfast or snack. They are the perfect meal to have before starting a long and busy day. Plus they will satisfy your sweet tooth and keep you energetic. Not to mention, your kids will love them too!

General Information:

Difficulty Level: *Medium*

Preparation Time: *5 min*

Cooking Time: *20 min*

Total Time Needed: *25 min*

Estimated Total Servings: *8*

Nutrition Facts:

Amount per serving:

Calories: *248*

Total Fat: *9.6 g*

Cholesterol: *47 mg*

Sodium: *174 mg*

Carbohydrate: *34.8 g*

Protein: *7.5 g*

Fiber: *4.5 g*

WW PointsPlus®: *7*

What You Need:

1 1/2 cups all-purpose whole wheat flour (about 6 3/4 ounces)

1 teaspoon baking powder

1/2 teaspoon baking soda

1/2 cup raw wheat germ

1/2 cup dried cranberries

1/2 teaspoon ground cinnamon

1/8 teaspoon ground nutmeg

1/4 teaspoon salt

2 large eggs

1/4 cup canola oil

1 teaspoon grated orange rind

1/2 cup freshly squeezed orange juice

1/2 cup brown sugar

Cooking spray

How to Make It:

Place the flour, baking powder, baking soda, wheat germ, dried cranberries, ground cinnamon, ground nutmeg and salt in a large bowl and mix well.

In a separate bowl, whisk together the eggs, canola oil, orange rind, juice and the brown sugar. Make a well in the middle of the dry ingredients mixture and add the egg mixture. Stir the wet and dry ingredients together just until they are blended. You want the mix to have a "chunky" consistency.

Preheat the oven to 370 degrees F (190 degrees C). Lightly grease 8 muffin tins with cooking spray. Spoon in the batter and divide evenly between the tins. Bake them for 18-20 minute or until a toothpick comes out clean when inserted into a muffin. Let them cool on a wire rack for a few minutes or enjoy them warm with some low-fat milk. Yum!

Tip: You can try different variations until you get your perfect sweet breakfast muffin: how about adding other fruits such as blueberries or bananas, or maybe some chopped pecans? This recipe is easy to make and truly versatile. You can even replace the brown sugar with some grated carrots and you just made healthy even healthier!

Homemade Cereal Bar

These delicious power bars are a perfect combination of crunchy and chewy. Plus, they're filling and can definitely satisfy your sweet tooth, and your need to stay energetic throughout the day. A great choice for a healthy breakfast, especially on those days when all you can do is grab something and go!

General Information:

Difficulty Level: *Difficult*

Preparation Time: *25 min*

Cooking Time: *30 min*

Total Time Needed: *55 min*

Estimated Total Servings: *8*

Nutrition Facts:

Amount per serving:

Calories: *244*

Total Fat: *10 g*

Cholesterol: *0 mg*

Sodium: *74 mg*

Carbohydrate: *38 g*

Protein: *5 g*

Fiber: *3 g*

WW PointsPlus®: *7*

What You Need:

1/4 cup slivered almonds

1 cup old-fashioned rolled oats

1 Tablespoon flaxseeds, preferably golden

1/4 cup sunflower seeds

1 Tablespoon sesame seeds

1/3 cup chopped dried apricots

1/3 cup currants

1/3 cup chopped golden raisins

1/2 teaspoon vanilla extract

1/4 cup brown sugar

1/4 cup raw honey

1/8 teaspoon salt

1/4 cup creamy all-natural almond butter

How to Make It:

Place the almonds, oats, flaxseeds, sun flower seeds and sesame seeds in a large rimmed baking tray and spread them evenly. Preheat the oven to 350 degrees F (175 degrees C) and bake the mixture for about 10 minutes - until the seeds are lightly toasted and the almonds have become deliciously fragrant. Halfway through the baking shake the tray to turn and move around the mixture.

Transfer the mixture to a large bowl and stir in the apricots, currants, and raisins.

In a small saucepan, blend together the vanilla, sugar, honey, salt and almond butter; set over low to medium heat and cook for about 4-5 minutes (the mixture should begin to bubble lightly on the surface); remember to stir often. Allow the mixture to cool off for a few minutes.

Once cooked, pour the almond butter mixture over the dry ingredients and stir well until the butter has coated all the dry ingredients.

Place the mix in a lightly greased 8 inch square pan and press it down until you obtain an even layer. You can use a little cooking spray to lightly grease your hands before proceeding to firmly press down the mixture or put some wax paper on top of the mixture while you press down. You want to make the mixture as tight as possible. Then place the pan in the refrigerator for about 30 minutes or until it becomes firm then cut into 8 cereal bars.

Tip: A great, satisfying breakfast that you can enjoy on the go, this delicious recipe is also versatile (as you can add or replace ingredients to fit your taste). It also freezes very well. Make it ahead of time and store it in the refrigerator or at

*room temperature in an air tight container for up to 1 week.
It is also the perfect take-along snack for work or school.*

English Maple Scones with a Twist

Best served on the day they are made, scones are an easy to make, yet fancy looking treat that you can have for breakfast or brunch; your entire family will enjoy this great recipe that it sweet while wonderfully complimenting any savory dishes or toppings that you serve it with.

General Information:

Difficulty Level: *Difficult*

Preparation Time: *20 min*

Cooking Time: *25 min*

Total Time Needed: *45 min*

Estimated Total Servings: *12*

Nutrition Facts:

Amount per serving:

Calories: *239*

Total Fat: *11.8 g*

Cholesterol: *14 mg*

Sodium: *133 mg*

Carbohydrate: *28.3 g*

Protein: *5.6 g*

Fiber: *2.2 g*

WW PointsPlus®: *6*

What You Need:

1 cup all-purpose flour

1 cup whole-wheat flour

1 cup old-fashioned rolled oats

1/4 cup plus 1 1/2 teaspoons brown sugar, divided

1/2 teaspoon baking soda

2 teaspoons baking powder

1 teaspoon ground cinnamon

1/4 teaspoon salt

2 Tablespoons chilled unsalted butter

4 Tablespoons reduced-fat cream cheese, cut into small pieces (2 ounces)

1/4 cup sunflower oil

1 cup diced peeled pear, preferably Bartlett (about 1 large pear)

1/2 cup chopped pecans, or walnuts, divided

3/4 cup low-fat buttermilk

1 teaspoon maple extract, or vanilla extract

1 egg lightly beaten with 1 Tablespoon water, for glaze

How to Make It:

Place the all-purpose flour, whole-wheat flour, oats, ¼ cup sugar, baking soda, baking powder, cinnamon and salt in a bowl and stir well. Using your hands, rub the butter and the cream cheese into the flour mixture. Add the sunflower oil and mix well. Also place the diced pear and ¼ cup nuts in the bowl and toss to coat them with the mixture.

Place the buttermilk and the maple or vanilla extract in a separate bowl, whisk them together and add to the mixture just enough to help form a sticky dough.

Flour a clean surface, place the dough on it and knead it for just 1 minute. Divide it in half and use your hands to pat each half into a 7 ½ -8 inches circle. Cut each circle into 6 wedges then transfer them to a baking sheet that you have already lined with wax paper. Brush each wedge with the egg-and-water mixture then sprinkle with the remaining nuts and press them in carefully.

Preheat the oven to 400 degrees F (210 degrees C) and bake the scones for about 25 minutes - they should become lightly golden and firm. Allow them to cool before serving.

Tip: Maple extract is sometimes hard to get, so do not worry if you cannot find it. Vanilla extract gives this dish an extraordinary taste, so use it with confidence. Also, keep in mind this is a "cheat day" meal or Sunday brunch indulgence. The recipe is modified from the classic cholesterol-infused scones, but it can easily become an unhealthy option. So keep portion size in check and accompany them with fresh fruit to keep your breakfast light.

Be Mine Blueberry Cake

Super healthy and easy to make, this is sure to become your favorite cake to have with coffee, tea or just to complete your breakfast. Sweet but not overly so, filling and nutritious, what more could you wish for? It's enough to feed the entire family, yet it leaves you feeling light and ready to face the day!

General Information:

Difficulty Level: *Medium*

Preparation Time: *20 min*

Cooking Time: *35 min*

Total Time Needed: *55 min*

Estimated Total Servings: *10*

Nutrition Facts:

Amount per serving:

Calories: *243*

Total Fat: *9.6 g*

Cholesterol: *39 mg*

Sodium: *285 mg*

Carbohydrate: *31.5 g*

Protein: *7.5 g*

Fiber: *1.6 g*

WW PointsPlus®: *6*

What You Need:

2 cups whole-wheat flour

1 teaspoon baking soda

1/2 teaspoon salt

1/2 cup chopped walnuts

1/2 teaspoon ground cinnamon

3 Tablespoons extra-virgin olive oil

1/2 cup brown sugar

2 large eggs

1 1/2 cup plain fat-free yogurt

1 teaspoon vanilla extract

Cooking spray

1 cup fresh blueberries, or frozen and thawed

How to Make It:

Place the whole-wheat flour, the baking soda and the salt in a bowl and mix them together. In a separate bowl, stir together the walnuts, 3 tablespoons from the brown sugar and the cinnamon.

In a third bowl, beat together the oil and the remaining brown sugar until the mixture becomes fluffy. Add the eggs one at a time and beat them in thoroughly, stirring <u>only</u> clockwise. Once the eggs are incorporated, blend in the non-fat yogurt and vanilla extract.

Add the flour mixture to the egg mixture in 2-3 batches to make it easier to blend. Stir thoroughly after adding each batch of flour.

Preheat the oven to 350 degrees F (175 degrees C) and use cooking spray to lightly grease an 8-inch square baking pan.

Place half of the batter in the pan and spread it evenly. Sprinkle it with half of the nut mixture and top with blueberries (lightly press them into the batter). Use a spoon to transfer the other half of the batter into the pan and sprinkle the rest of the nut mixture on top.

Bake the cake for about 30 minutes or until a toothpick comes out clean when inserted in the center. Allow the cake to cool completely before cutting it into 10 square pieces.

Tip: This great breakfast treat keeps well, so store the cake pieces in an air tight container and enjoy for several days. To add more flavor you can throw in some golden raisins in the nut mixture or replace the blueberries with grated apples.

Winter Oatmeal

Simple and delicious, this oatmeal recipe is a great choice to keep you and those around you healthy. Plus it's the perfect meal to get you energized for a busy day, while making sure you get a well balanced breakfast and a dash of sweetness right from the get go.

General Information:

Difficulty Level: *Easy*

Preparation Time: *10 min*

Cooking Time: *10 min*

Total Time Needed: *20 min*

Estimated Total Servings: *4*

Nutrition Facts:

Amount per serving:

Calories: *296*

Total Fat: *13.4 g*

Cholesterol: *3 mg*

Sodium: *182 mg*

Carbohydrate: *38.8 g*

Protein: *8.4 g*

Fiber: *5.7 g*

WW PointsPlus®: *8*

What You Need:

1/4 teaspoon salt, optional

3 1/2 cups water

2 cups old-fashioned oats

1/2 cup pecans, coarsely chopped

Pinch nutmeg

1/4 teaspoon vanilla extract

2 Tablespoons dark brown sugar

1 cup low fat milk, divided

1 teaspoon ground cinnamon

1/2 cup green grapes

How to Make It:

Place the salt and water in a medium sized saucepan and bring to a boil over medium heat. Add the raisins and oats, stir well then reduce heat and allow the mixture to simmer uncovered for 5-6 minutes, stirring from time to time.

Meanwhile, place the nuts in a medium sized skillet, set it over high heat and toast until they become golden and have a delicious nutty fragrance to them - it should take approximately 5-6 minutes.

Once the oats are ready, remove from heat, add the nutmeg and the vanilla extract then stir thoroughly. Sprinkle the brown sugar then transfer into serving bowls. Add ¼ cup of milk to every bowl and top everything with the toasted nuts and ground cinnamon.

Tip: This is an amazing recipe that you can build on and experiment with until you find your perfect oat meal. Feel free to try cranberries, blueberries, peaches, apple slices (or even apple sauce) or almonds.

Guilt-Free Breakfast Mini Pizzas

Pizza for breakfast, that's right - and by right we mean healthy, nutritious and delicious! These easy to make mini pizzas are rich in proteins and vitamins, filling and tasty. Oh, and did we mention it is pizza? Dig in and enjoy it with a clear conscience.

General Information:

Difficulty Level: *Medium*

Preparation Time: *10 min*

Cooking Time: *30 min*

Total Time Needed: *40 min*

Estimated Total Servings: *4*

Nutrition Facts:

Amount per serving:

Calories: *267*

Total Fat: *9.8 g*

Cholesterol: *58 mg*

Sodium: *835 mg*

Carbohydrate: *28.8 g*

Protein: *17.5 g*

Fiber: *3.3 g*

WW PointsPlus®: *7*

What You Need:

4 lean ground turkey sausage links

4 whole wheat 6-inch pitas

4 egg whites

1/2 cup fat-free milk

1/8 teaspoon pepper

2 Tablespoons grated Parmesan cheese

1/2 cup (2 oz) shredded 2% reduced-fat sharp Cheddar cheese

1 1/2 cups pizza sauce

2 teaspoons oregano (optional)

How to Make It:

Set a pan over medium heat. Cut each sausage link in about 6 round pieces. Cook the sausages until the inside is no longer pink - it should take about 10-12 minutes. Transfer it onto paper towels and pat dry to get rid of as much excess fat as possible.

While the sausages are cooking whisk together the egg whites, milk, pepper and parmesan cheese. Place a large skillet over medium heat. Cook the mixture for about 3-4 minutes while stirring the eggs every 30 seconds to cook through.

Spread 1/4 cup pizza sauce on each pita. Divide the egg mixture and shredded cheddar in 4 equal portions. Lay the scrambled eggs on top of each pita, then add the sausages and sprinkle the cheese. Add 1 Tablespoon pizza sauce on top of the cheese.

Preheat the oven to 375 degrees F (190 degrees C) and bake the mini pizzas until the cheese melts and the egg starts getting golden brown margins. It should take no longer than 15-20 minutes.

Sprinkle with oregano and serve them warm.

Tip: If there are any ingredients that you love on your pizza, feel free to add them. How about mushrooms, onion, and some green pepper? Add them to the eggs or just before you bake the pizza, to keep the taste fresh.

Healthy Frenchy

French toast is one of the favorite Sunday brunch meals for adults and kids alike! It's time to rediscover the joys of this tasty treat in a low calorie, flavorful way! This recipe re-invents the classic, by making it kids-friendly and heart healthy!

General Information:

Difficulty Level: *Easy*

Preparation Time: *5 min*

Cooking Time: *25 min*

Total Time Needed: *30 min*

Estimated Total Servings: *4*

Nutrition Facts:

Amount per serving:

Calories: *247*

Total Fat: *3.6 g*

Cholesterol: *42 mg*

Sodium: *450 mg*

Carbohydrate: *47.7 g*

Protein: *12.2 g*

Fiber: *7.9 g*

WW PointsPlus®: *7*

What You Need:

1 egg

2 egg whites

1/4 cup 2% milk

1 Tablespoon vanilla extract

8 slices 100% whole wheat bread

2 teaspoons raw honey

1 cup fresh strawberries

How to Make It:

In a medium bowl beat the egg and egg whites together. In a separate bowl, whisk milk and vanilla extract together.

Heat a non-stick griddle or pan over medium heat. Dip each slice of bread in the vanilla milk, then coat it with the eggs mixture and place it in the pan. Cook for about 2-3 minutes on each side until it becomes golden brown. Repeat until all the slices are cooked.

Slice each strawberry in half. Top each toast with a bit of honey and 5-6 strawberry halves.

Tip: Looking to give this dish a flavor kick? Try sprinkling some lemon zest and cinnamon along with the honey. You won't believe how flavorful this little trick can be!

How You Are Making a Difference

I am a true believer in giving back. Whether it's time, money or a smile, I believe we all have the power to make somebody's day better and help those who need it. Just because **you are so awesome** and you invested in your health, I want you to know that I trully support that.

You are not only helping yourself by eating healthier, you are also helping others: a percentage of all the proceeds from this cookbook will be given to support Oprah Winfrey's Angel Network Chairties. She is one amazing lady, who has been inspiring the world for so many years, and her organization supports education, women, the community and human rights, all the things I believe in and support.

Your good deed deserves another, and this is my way of doing that good deed.

Corina Tudose

Thank You

Thank you for reading *Healthy Breakfasts Under 300 Calories Cookbook* and investing in *your* health. I hope you and your entire family enjoy making and eating these delicious dishes. If you liked this book, please take a few moments to leave a review. I always appreciate feedback and positive feedback really makes my day!

Do you have questions about how to transform your favorite dish into a healthy meal? Here is how you can get in touch with me:

- Visit http://www.Healthyvore.com/blog for a ton of delicious recipes and healthy tips.

- Like Healthyvore on Facebook http://www.facebook.com/Healthyvore for instant access to a community dedicated to eating and living healthy.

- As a bonus for getting my book, I am giving you the "7 Ways To Instantly Boost Your Energy" e-book for FREE. To get instant access and your free download visit the special VIP link below: http://www.healthyvore.com/vip/

I'd love to hear from you!

All the best,

Corina Tudose

About the Author

Corina Tudose is a certified Fitness and Nutrition Coach and the founder of Healthyvore, a corporate wellness consulting firm specializing in helping businesses design effective and efficient wellness cultures. You can follow Corina on Twitter (@healthyvore) and on her blog (http://www.healthyvore.com/blog).

Corina has always been passionate about food and cooking. In her own words:

"I grew up seeing my mother and my grandmother cook. I could never understand how from a bunch of "nothing" they can create such amazing dishes. Honestly, Math seemed a lot less complex than cooking. Until one day, when I picked up a cookbook and gave it a try.

Ever since then, I see cooking as a form of art and creativity. It's the one time I can play and be inventive. The one time I escape from the seriousness of it all and "make something out of nothing". It's an amazing feeling. I might not be able to build a bridge, or fly a plane, but I can assure you, I can prepare a heck of a meal!"

Corina believes in cooking with natural ingredients, which fuel the body with energy and keep us healthy and strong to face our everyday challenges.

Other Works by Corina Tudose

The Amazon Bestseller:

SNACKS UNDER 100 CALORIES

That Keep You Feeling Full and Help You Lose Weight

Get your copy by visiting:

http://www.healthyvore.com/books.html

34367463R00053

Made in the USA
Middletown, DE
21 August 2016